# Reggie Miller

## Additional Titles in the Sports Reports Series

**Andre Agassi**
Star Tennis Player
(0-89490-798-0)

**Troy Aikman**
Star Quarterback
(0-89490-927-4)

**Roberto Alomar**
Star Second Baseman
(0-7660-1079-1)

**Charles Barkley**
Star Forward
(0-89490-655-0)

**Jeff Gordon**
Star Race Car Driver
(0-7660-1083-X)

**Wayne Gretzky**
Star Center
(0-89490-930-4)

**Ken Griffey, Jr.**
Star Outfielder
(0-89490-802-2)

**Scott Hamilton**
Star Figure Skater
(0-7660-1236-0)

**Anfernee Hardaway**
Star Guard
(0-7660-1234-4)

**Grant Hill**
Star Forward
(0-7660-1078-3)

**Michael Jordan**
Star Guard
(0-89490-482-5)

**Shawn Kemp**
Star Forward
(0-89490-929-0)

**Mario Lemieux**
Star Center
(0-89490-932-0)

**Karl Malone**
Star Forward
(0-89490-931-2)

**Dan Marino**
Star Quarterback
(0-89490-933-9)

**Mark McGwire**
Star Home Run Hitter
(0-7660-1329-4)

**Mark Messier**
Star Center
(0-89490-801-4)

**Reggie Miller**
Star Guard
(0-7660-1082-1)

**Chris Mullin**
Star Forward
(0-89490-486-8)

**Hakeem Olajuwon**
Star Center
(0-89490-803-0)

**Shaquille O'Neal**
Star Center
(0-89490-656-9)

**Scottie Pippen**
Star Forward
(0-7660-1080-5)

**Cal Ripken, Jr.**
Star Shortstop
(0-89490-485-X)

**David Robinson**
Star Center
(0-89490-483-3)

**Barry Sanders**
Star Running Back
(0-89490-484-1)

**Deion Sanders**
Star Athlete
(0-89490-652-6)

**Junior Seau**
Star Linebacker
(0-89490-800-6)

**Emmitt Smith**
Star Running Back
(0-89490-653-4)

**Frank Thomas**
Star First Baseman
(0-89490-659-3)

**Thurman Thomas**
Star Running Back
(0-89490-445-0)

**Chris Webber**
Star Forward
(0-89490-799-9)

**Tiger Woods**
Star Golfer
(0-7660-1081-3)

**Steve Young**
Star Quarterback
(0-89490-654-2)

**Jim Kelly**
Star Quarterback
(0-89490-446-9)

**Jerry Rice**
Star Wide Receiver
(0-89490-928-2)

SPORTS REPORTS

# Reggie Miller

## Star Guard

Peter C. Bjarkman

**Enslow Publishers, Inc.**

40 Industrial Road         PO Box 38
Box 398                Aldershot
Berkeley Heights, NJ 07922    Hants GU12 6BP
USA                          UK
http://www.enslow.com

*Dedicated to MaryKay Hruskocy, who remains
one of the Indiana Pacers' most professional "players."*

**Library of Congress Cataloging-in-Publication Data**

Bjarkman, Peter C.
     Reggie Miller: star guard / Peter C. Bjarkman.
        p.  cm. — (Sports reports)
     Includes bibliographical references (p.  ) and index.
     Summary: Examines the life and career of the popular basketball
star Reggie Miller, known as one of the best shooters in the game.
     ISBN 0-7660-1082-1
     1. Miller, Reggie, 1965–  —Juvenile literature. 2. Basketball
players—United States—Biography—Juvenile literature.
[1. Miller, Reggie, 1965–  . 2. Basketball players. 3. Afro-Americans
—Biography.] I. Title. II. Series.
GV884.M556B53   1999
796.323'092—dc21
    [B]                              98-33312
                                        CIP
                                        AC

Printed in the United States of America

10 9 8 7 6 5 4 3 2 1

**To Our Readers:**
All Internet addresses in this book were active and appropriate when we went to
press. Any comments or suggestions can be sent by e-mail to Comments@enslow.com
or to the address on the back cover.

**Photo Credits:** Frank P. McGrath, Jr., pp. 6, 13, 26, 38, 41, 46, 47, 53, 56, 64,
72, 74, 79, 84, 88, 93, 97; Sports Information Department, University of
Southern California, pp. 24, 32.

**Cover Photo:** Frank P. McGrath, Jr.

# Contents

*Reggie Miller displayed his jump shots during a game against the Atlanta Hawks, only a few weeks after a severe eye injury almost ended his career.*

# Chapter 1

# Reggie, Reggie!

In mid-April of 1996 the career of NBA superstar Reggie Miller nearly came to a sudden, horrifying end. Two weeks before the much-anticipated National Basketball Association (NBA) playoffs, the Indiana Pacers star guard was poked in the eye and suffered a painful fractured eye socket. With only four games remaining in the regular season and the Pacers within four victories of matching their best season ever, Miller had suffered an injury that threatened to put an immediate end to his team's playoff hopes.

The disastrous moment came in the first quarter of a tense game against the Detroit Pistons in Market Square Arena. Diving for a loose ball, Miller collided violently with Otis Thorpe and Allan Houston. It was the Pacers' star who received most of the impact from the three-man collision, and Miller fell backward in agony. He remained on the floor for five minutes, twisting in pain and clutching his head while a doctor and team trainer quickly applied first aid. He never lost consciousness, despite suffering blurred vision, a mild concussion, and a sprained neck from the crushing collision. X rays taken after Miller was rushed to Indianapolis's St. Vincent Hospital revealed a fracture to the eye socket. Doctors quickly decided surgery would be needed.

Dr. John Abrams, an eye doctor and a member of the Pacers' medical team, explained the details of Reggie Miller's condition in a press conference. He assured fans, reporters, and team officials that this was a common injury in the NBA, "because of the makeup of the game, the elbows, and the force you can create into the eye orbit."[1] Dr. Michael Welsh, who performed the surgery, told anxious listeners that Miller was just as likely to recover fully as several other NBA players who had earlier suffered similar injuries but later resumed their athletic careers.

Everyone was relieved to learn that Miller's vision would not be permanently damaged. The news was not entirely good, however, for a team about to enter the postseason and now deprived of its top star for at least several weeks. There was serious doubt whether Indiana's star player could return in time to lead his team to another playoff run.

There was even some doubt whether Miller would ever play basketball effectively again. He was a deadly long-range shooter, and long-range shooting seemed to require clear vision as well as a soft shooting touch. In the biggest games it was Miller's ability to make the crucial baskets that usually kept the Pacers in contention. Reggie Miller is one of the league's grittiest competitors. He is one player who never gives up when facing defeat and never backs away from any large challenge.

Few among the Pacers' faithful were surprised when in only a few short weeks Reggie Miller was making a most miraculous comeback. With his team facing first-round elimination by the tough Atlanta Hawks, Miller returned to the floor at Market Square Arena for Game 5 of the opening playoff series. It was just twenty-two days after his collision and eye surgery. No one had counted on Indiana's top player being back in action quite this soon. He returned to an excited reception from enthusiastic Indiana fans. In typical Miller fashion, he somehow provided one of the greatest clutch performances of his already brilliant career.

When Reggie Miller was announced in the starting lineup for Game 5, a packed coliseum greeted its hero with a deafening ovation that seemed to shake the walls of Market Square Arena. Still suffering from blurred vision, Miller responded with a game-long shooting clinic that rewrote the team's and the league's record books. He played with tinted goggles to protect his injured eye from both bright lights and any further damaging blows. He quickly began throwing in shots that seemed guided by radar. Before the thrilling game was over, he banged in 29 points, including 16 during the dramatic fourth quarter. He was 13 for 15 from the free-throw line, with 11 of his 13 free shots made in the exciting final period. His free-throw effort in the fourth period was only two shots short of a league record held by Chicago's Michael Jordan.

Despite Reggie Miller's heroics, the Pacers fell short by a mere two points to lose the game that ended their season. It was a disappointing finale for a team that had begun the year with so much optimism. The Pacers had even appeared ready to climb beyond the first round of the playoffs and compete for the NBA championship. But it was a most dramatic way to end the season nonetheless. The Pacers would again have to wait at least another year for a chance at winning the championship. Yet Miller, for

# STATS

Reggie Miller is the Indiana Pacers' career leader in all but a few statistical categories. Only in rebounds, blocked shots, steals, and assists is he not first on the team's all-time list. Here are some of Miller's standings in the Indiana Pacers' record book as of the end of the 1997–98 season:

| STATISTICAL CATEGORY | CAREER TOTALS | REGGIE'S RANKING |
| --- | --- | --- |
| Points Scored | 17,402 | 1st |
| Scoring Average | 19.7 | 1st |
| Field Goals Made | 5,695 | 1st |
| 3-Pt. Field Goals Made | 1,596 | 1st |
| Free Throws Made | 4,416 | 1st |
| Assists | 2,764 | 2nd* |
| Steals | 1,037 | 2nd** |
| Seasons Played | 11 | 1st*** |
| Games Played | 882 | 1st |
| Minutes Played | 30,299 | 1st |

*behind Vern Fleming    **behind Don Buse    ***tied with Vern Fleming his part, had again made a clear statement to NBA fans and opponents around the league. The Indiana Pacers' clutch-shooting star was certainly one of the pro league's most dangerous playoff performers.

The ongoing love affair between Miller and his thousands of Indiana Pacers fans is as impressive as anything found within the glamorous NBA. Even Michael Jordan in Chicago never quite topped the adoration that Reggie Miller draws time and again from his Indianapolis supporters. That love for the star local player truly reached a fever pitch in Indianapolis by the end of the 1996 basketball season.

The honeymoon between Reggie Miller and his hometown fans continued in the months that followed. He performed heroically for America's Dream Team III squad during the Olympic Games in Atlanta, Georgia. Miller was the top three-point shooter and one of the most durable players for a star-studded USA team. With Miller as the fourth-best scorer, America's Dream Team easily won an expected Olympic gold medal. For the Indianapolis fans, Reggie Miller's Olympic success was a long-overdue recognition that the Pacers' star was among the league's very brightest celebrities—equal to Charles Barkley, Patrick Ewing, David Robinson, and even Michael Jordan and Shaquille O'Neal.

*Rookie Reggie Miller is defended by Boston Celtics' star Larry Bird, who would become Miller's coach at Indiana eleven seasons later.*

As popular as Miller was with the Indianapolis crowds immediately after his heroics that closed the 1996 basketball season, this mutual love affair with hometown Indiana fans was not always at such a high peak. In fact, Miller's Indianapolis career began nine years earlier on something of a low note. And there would also be many ups and downs to follow, even in the years after he became a recognized NBA star.

The Pacers' selection of the University of California at Los Angeles (UCLA) All-American with their eleventh overall draft pick in June 1987 was not a popular move with Indianapolis fans. They wanted the Pacers to draft another guard, Steve Alford.[2] Alford had been a star at nearby Indiana University. Before that, he had been a local high school hero in the basketball-crazy Hoosier State. Alford was one of the most popular players of all time in Indiana. Miller had led his UCLA team to victory over Alford and the hometown Hoosiers during the year-end 1985 National Invitational Tournament.

Nonetheless, Miller quickly converted the local fans with spectacular play during his rookie NBA season. Within three seasons he was one of the highest scorers and deadliest shooters in franchise history. Meanwhile, Alford did little during brief stays with teams in both Dallas and San Francisco.

Reggie Miller turned fans around completely during the next decade. Unfortunately, he seemed to lose them again. Ironically, his downfall began almost at the very moment he reached peak popularity with his playoff heroics against Atlanta. Before the year was out, there would be a series of incidents that caused Miller's popular image to slide dramatically with the hometown fans.

First came his much-publicized holdout for a new contract with a large salary increase that very same summer. There was also an unfortunate television interview where Miller seemed to indicate that he did not want to play anymore in Indianapolis and that he would only be satisfied with a deal for $10 million per season.[3] Overnight, Reggie Miller was appearing to be just another selfish and money-hungry superstar.

In the following NBA season, Miller again played well but could not redeem himself simply because the Pacers team as a whole failed so miserably. The team lost more games than it won and failed to return to the year-end playoffs.

A final blow came when Miller's house burned to the ground in an unexplained case of arson. Only weeks after the 1997 season ended, someone set a fire that destroyed the 14,000-square-foot dream home that Miller and his wife, Marita, had just finished building in one of the most exclusive neighborhoods outside Indianapolis.[4] Miller was crushed and even considered retiring from basketball.

The fire caused fear and mistrust on the part of the Pacers star. It seemed to cap off the rough times that had plagued him during the year that followed his Olympic triumphs. After the fire at his house, Miller was far less trusting of crowds and even began appearing in public with a bodyguard at his side. Many Pacers followers were shocked, because Miller had always been one of the players most willing to mix freely with the fans. It was an unfortunate new image for the Indiana Pacers fan favorite.

But Reggie Miller has always rebounded from even the greatest adversities. As a youngster, he had beaten odds that said he would never be able to walk and run like other kids. He eventually outlived the early embarrassment of his hometown reputation as a high school player who was not as talented as his own superstar sister. And he would eventually win back the hearts of Indianapolis fans when a revitalized Indiana Pacers team would once again challenge for an NBA championship.

# Chapter 2

# Beaten by Your Big Sister

**N**o superstar athlete of recent decades comes from a more talented athletic family than Reggie Miller. And no other NBA star has overcome more obstacles along the way to athletic fame and fortune. As a youngster, Reggie first had to battle against a birth defect that threatened to leave him crippled and housebound. His hips had a defect that caused his legs to be unable to move freely. One way to recover was to spend hours practicing on the basketball court with his athletically talented sister Cheryl. The rivalry of those backyard games helped young Reggie regain his full physical strength. The same competitions also set up his next big personal obstacle. Reggie was one future NBA star who, for years, had to struggle on the backyard court just to beat his own sister.

When a basketball player makes it in the NBA, he is normally "top dog" in his own family, as well as in his own hometown and on the college campus where he developed his skills. For a rare few, being a big-time sports star is not necessarily enough to become the main celebrity in the neighborhood or even in the family.

Miller is one of those few unlucky celebrities who had to live in the shadow of a parent, a brother, or a sister who earned still-greater fame or displayed superior talent. This position is not always a bad thing, however. Reggie's exceptionally close family took pride in each other's achievements. There was no jealousy between famous brothers and sisters. For Reggie, the presence of family members who were also in the spotlight was an early source of his own inspiration and drive to succeed.[1]

In the Miller family there was always more than enough talent to go around, starting with Reggie's dad, Saul. He was a sports star in both high school and college, but also had other gifts and interests that led to successes in many areas.

Growing up in Memphis, Tennessee, in the 1950s, Saul Miller was so good on the local Jefferson High School basketball team that he was named a schoolboy All-American. When he attended Southern Illinois University, he was an all-conference basketball player. Saul Miller was also talented as a musician, and music, not sports, would prove to be his main love.

A skilled saxophone player, Saul Miller played with some of the country's best jazz bands. He moved to California to pursue his musical career. There he performed with such musical headliners as Lionel Hampton and B. B. King. He joined the Air Force, where he pursued a career as a computer programmer. While in the Air Force, Miller continued to play his sax. It was during a gig with the renowned Phineas Newborn quartet back in his hometown of Memphis that Saul first met his future wife, Carrie.

After Saul and Carrie were married, they traveled back to California, where Carrie became a registered nurse, and Saul reenlisted with the Air Force. It was a career he would follow for two decades, before he retired in 1977 with the rank of Chief Master Sergeant. It was a career that would keep him at March Air Force Base near Riverside, California, where the last three of five Miller children were born. Saul and Carrie's oldest child is Saul, Jr., born in Memphis shortly after his father's reenlistment. Darrell was born in Washington, D.C.

Then came Cheryl in 1964, Reggie a year later, and finally the youngest child, Tammy.

The oldest brother of the Miller clan would follow in his father's footsteps, both as a musician and a military man. Saul, Jr., would one day perform with the Airmen of Note, the best and most famous jazz band sponsored by the United States Air Force. Darrell also followed his father's footsteps, but on the athletic field, not in the music field. Darrell's sport was baseball, although he was also a multisport star while in high school at Riverside. Darrell's baseball talents would enable him to make it to the big leagues as a catcher and outfielder with the nearby California Angels. When his five years as a major-league ballplayer were over in 1988, Darrell moved to the team's front office. Today he is a top scout for the Angels and covers the southern California and Arizona regions.

Darrell was a role model for the three youngest Millers: Reggie and his two sisters. They spent hours competing on the family's makeshift driveway basketball court. Tammy eventually preferred volleyball and became a star player of that sport at California State College in Fullerton, where she studied law. Cheryl and Reggie were left to follow their father's passion and talent for basketball. For a long while, it was Cheryl who drew all the attention,

# FACT

Reggie Miller's family is filled with remarkable performing talent, with two brothers starring as professional athletes, two sisters excelling as college athletes, and a third brother and a father whose talents included both sports and music.

| | |
|---|---|
| **Cheryl** | Member of Naismith Basketball Hall of Fame |
| **Reggie** | NBA star with Indiana Pacers |
| **Darrell** | Big league baseball player with California Angels |
| **Tammy** | Volleyball player at Cal State-Fullerton and later a lawyer |
| **Saul, Jr.** | Musician with U.S. Airmen of Note jazz band |
| **Saul, Sr.** | High school basketball All-American and top jazz band performer |

once she became a superstar on the school women's team at Riverside Polytechnic High. By the time Reggie made it to high school, he had a brother who was playing professional baseball in the minor leagues and a sister who was threatening to become a high school legend on the basketball courts.

But Reggie had to surpass much more than the reputations of talented brothers and sisters before he could be a star athlete. First, he had to overcome handicaps that threatened to rob him of a normal life. Reggie was born so crippled that he could not run and play like the other children in his family and his neighborhood.

"My mother cried when I was born," Miller recalled, "I came out with my legs and hips all contorted and twisted, like someone had tried to tie me in a knot. The doctors said I might not ever walk and [not to] think about playing sports. . . . That was August 24, 1965."[2] Because of the  birth defect, the youngest Miller boy had to wear steel braces on his legs until he was four. He would sit in the kitchen with his mom and watch the others play on the driveway basketball court. Reggie Miller remembers that his mom never gave up hope for a minute that he would soon be joining his brothers and sisters in their backyard games. Carrie Miller believed totally in her son's full recovery. She never doubted he would get strong enough to romp in the family games. Soon Reggie was indeed out there with the others.

When Reggie did start to join those family contests in the driveway, there was a new challenge to be faced. That challenge was sister Cheryl. It was Cheryl who had the neighborhood talking about her early rare basketball talent. She could beat anyone in town at one-on-one. And she was the one that got most of Saul Miller's coaching attention. When the family moved to a new house in Riverside, California, Saul built a brand-new court in the backyard, this time dug into the side of a hill. Saul trained his daughter religiously and had Reggie help out by playing defense.[3]

Miller remembers his sister dominating him in every game they played. It can be embarrassing to a young athlete when his sister slams down every one of his own shots, but Reggie knew that Cheryl could do exactly the same thing to everyone else on the block and anywhere else in town. "One of the reasons I practiced shooting from the outside," Reggie recalls, "was that Cheryl used to block my shots when I drove to the hoop. It's a bad feeling when your sister is knocking your best stuff into the rosebushes."[4]

Of course, sometimes a sister who can beat all the boys in town on the basketball court is a definite plus. Reggie would later boast of the days when he would approach guys shooting in the park and ask, "Wanna play me and my sister for ten bucks?" As Reggie remembered, "Cheryl would come out of the bushes. Boom, boom, she'd shoot and we'd win. The guys would be awed."[5]

Beating Cheryl in their backyard contests eventually became Reggie's obsession. He would relentlessly practice the style of shooting that he had

*Reggie Miller spent years playing in the shadow of his sister Cheryl, who once scored 105 points in a high school game.*

learned from his father. Reggie's father showed him the way to make sure he followed up every shot—how to hold his hand when releasing the ball and then keep the hand raised after the ball left his fingers.[6] Reggie would practice between five hundred and seven hundred shots each day. He would practice his shots from every angle and from farther and farther out. Soon he was tossing them from the middle of his mom's flowerbeds, something his mother did not much appreciate. His father had to add new cement and lengthen the backyard court on several occasions.

Reggie was not a promising future star like Cheryl when he tried out for the high school team at Riverside Polytechnic. He was a skinny kid who weighed only 140 pounds and stood only five feet nine inches. He drank milk and ate endlessly, hoping he could gain a few pounds or, better, grow a few inches. Reggie could not dunk the ball until he was a sophomore. But he was always improving his long-range shot. He was much quicker than other kids, despite his weak legs as a child. And he was developing a mental attitude that was very tough and very disciplined. Five to seven hundred shots each day on the practice court developed plenty of discipline.

Reggie sat on the bench all year as a freshman,

*Reggie Miller today displays the determination he acquired as a young boy in backyard contests with his sister.*

something else that can help a player develop plenty of self-discipline. When he began getting a chance to play in his sophomore year, however, his family gave the same support to Reggie that they did to Cheryl. Their father would attend all of Cheryl's games, partly because he served as an unofficial trainer for the Riverside girls' team. He taped the players' ankles before all their games. If Reggie had

## FACT

Cheryl Miller, a member of the Naismith Memorial Basketball Hall of Fame, is said by many to be the greatest women's player of all time. Her career at USC included the following achievements:

- Four-time All-American (1983–1986).
- Three-time Naismith College Player of the Year (1984–1986).
- Led USC to two NCAA National Championships (1983, 1984).
- Named 1980s Player of the Decade by United States Basketball Writers Association.
- USC career leader in points, rebounds, field goals, free throws, and steals.
- Scored California state record 105 points in a high school game.
- First (male or female) *Parade* magazine four-time high school All-American.
- Only (male or female) USC basketball player to have uniform number retired.

a game the same night as Cheryl, however, he did not have to go alone. Reggie's mother would always be in the stands to root on her son.

One night during his first season of playing regularly, Reggie scored 39 points and both son and mother gleefully rushed home to inform the family of his sudden success. He was convinced he now could play the game just like Cheryl. But when they arrived home to join Saul and Cheryl who had just returned from the girls' contest, it was only to discover that Cheryl had that very night set a state record by scoring an incredible 105 points. Nonetheless, the family was just as proud of Reggie's more modest achievement as they were of Cheryl's remarkable one. They were that kind of close-knit family and there was no room for jealousy in the Miller household. Reggie, too, was proud of Cheryl's record and not at all dismayed that she had once again shown him up.[7] In fact, Reggie still says that Cheryl's record-breaking game that night was one of the biggest thrills of his lifetime.

# Chapter 3

# Just Another UCLA Bruins Legend

**R**eggie Miller's basketball career began almost by accident. By the start of his sophomore year of high school, the skinny kid from Riverside had grown a couple of inches. With all the practice on the family backyard court, he had also learned to shoot a real jump shot. Before, he had heaved the ball while standing still, with an awkward one-handed set shot that began down by his hips.[1] Reggie's dad taught him the proper style for a true jumper and also encouraged him always to stay mentally ready in case the coach's call came for him to play. But Reggie was not very optimistic. Despite the extra height and his improved shot, he was still a lowly substitute buried deep on the bench.

Then a truly strange thing occurred. Moments before a road game, it was discovered that one of the starting players for Riverside Poly had accidentally brought his white home uniform instead of the required dark road uniform. The star forward would therefore not be able to play in this game. Coach Arlo Gard scanned the locker room and reluctantly announced that Miller would have to start in his place. As Miller remembered it, Coach Gard was not very enthusiastic about the prospect of using his untested sophomore.[2] But the accident had, nonetheless, provided the skinny substitute with a rare chance to play.

When the break came, Reggie Miller was more than ready. All that backyard shooting practice would now have a chance to pay off. The first few minutes of the game Miller was confused and felt awkward. He dropped a pass and missed his first shots badly. Soon, though, he was able to relax, and his shots began to fall just as they always had at home. Miller had practiced so much that shooting was second nature even if being in a real game felt strange. When the final buzzer sounded, Reggie Miller's team had won, and the unexpected starter for Riverside Poly had thrown down 35 points.

Miller remembers the lesson he learned that night about being prepared, the lesson that Saul, Sr., had repeated so many times. Coach Gard had a new starter and the very next game Reggie pumped in 45 points. He was even chosen as player of the week by the local press. Reggie Miller was never a sub or a benchwarmer again at Riverside Polytechnic High School. Nor was Miller ever again unprepared for the challenges that fate and circumstances might toss his way.

Basketball was not the original game of choice for the youngest of the Miller boys. At first, Reggie had wanted to follow brother Darrell on the baseball field. As a freshman, he also played the slower-paced game of baseball at Riverside Poly. He spent hours playing corkball with neighborhood kids, a game in which the "ball" was a cork from a wine bottle and the "bat" was a broom handle. Then, one day, Reggie suddenly realized that baseball was lacking something he wanted and needed from playing team sports.

"I was standing in the outfield one day and it was cold. The wind was whistling, and nobody was hitting the ball to me. That's when I decided I needed something nonstop. I needed that excitement, that adrenaline to get me going."[3]

Reggie Miller got off the bench as a sophomore. He still did not get out from behind Cheryl's growing shadow, however. He might have been a

*Cheryl Miller is a member of the Naismith Memorial Basketball Hall of Fame and is considered by many to be the greatest women's college basketball player of all time.*

surprising choice for local player of the week early in his second season, but his sister was already regarded as the best women's player in the entire country. She was well on her way to four straight selections as a *Parade* magazine high school All-American, the first male or female player ever to win that honor. Reggie would himself be a star of major proportions by the time he was a senior. He led his Riverside Poly team to a California divisional championship and was selected as the state's best male player. But Cheryl's women's team won 132 of 136 games during the same seasons. Cheryl was the only high school star in the land to be named to the women's USA National Team during her senior season, which was also Reggie's junior year.

Both Cheryl and Reggie had many college scholarship offers to choose from. Cheryl decided to enter the University of Southern California (USC) at the start of Reggie's senior season at Riverside. Reggie knew that he would have to go elsewhere if he was ever to be judged by his own achievements and not Cheryl's. Reggie settled on another local college, UCLA.

Reggie Miller's choice of college was not based on basketball alone, though UCLA certainly boasted one of the finest basketball reputations in the nation. He

# STATS

UCLA has won more national championships in basketball than any other school. Here is a list of championship years, coaches, records, star UCLA players, and their points per game (ppg).

| YEAR | TITLE | COACH | RECORD | STAR PLAYER | PPG |
|------|-------|-------|--------|-------------|-----|
| 1964 | NCAA | John Wooden | 30–0 | Walt Hazzard | 18.6 |
| 1965 | NCAA | John Wooden | 28–2 | Gail Goodrich | 24.8 |
| 1967 | NCAA | John Wooden | 30–0 | Lew Alcindor* | 29.0 |
| 1968 | NCAA | John Wooden | 29–1 | Lew Alcindor | 26.2 |
| 1969 | NCAA | John Wooden | 29–1 | Lew Alcindor | 24.0 |
| 1970 | NCAA | John Wooden | 28–2 | Sidney Wicks | 18.6 |
| 1971 | NCAA | John Wooden | 29–1 | Sidney Wicks | 21.3 |
| 1972 | NCAA | John Wooden | 30–0 | Bill Walton | 21.1 |
| 1973 | NCAA | John Wooden | 30–0 | Bill Walton | 20.4 |
| 1975 | NCAA | John Wooden | 28–3 | Rich Washington | 15.9 |
| 1985 | NIT | Walt Hazzard | 21–12 | Reggie Miller | 15.2 |
| 1995 | NCAA | Jim Harrick | 31–2 | Ed O'Bannon | 20.4 |

*Later changed name to Kareem Abdul-Jabbar*

also had dreams of acting and wanted to study theater in college. UCLA had a top drama program.

At UCLA Miller would not yet be free of comparisons to his famous sister. While he was a freshman substitute, again struggling to make the starting team, she was leading her USC ballclub to a national championship. When he was a starter after the middle of his sophomore year, the newspapers and magazines were writing that he was the first UCLA player who probably could not beat his sister at one-on-one.[4]

And Cheryl was not the only shadow hovering over Reggie's head in those first seasons on the UCLA campus. This was the proudest basketball school in the country. Under legendary coach John Wooden the school had only ten years earlier accomplished a feat never duplicated—winning seven National Collegiate Athletic Association (NCAA) championships in a row. The Bruins captured the national championship tournament ten times in twelve seasons between 1964 and 1975.

Some of the greatest players in history had played for UCLA. There was the great center Lew Alcindor, who would later change his name to Kareem Abdul-Jabbar when he played for the pros. There was another great center, Bill Walton, some say the best ever. College basketball fans were still arguing whether it was Alcindor or Walton who was the greatest college basketball player of all time.

Reggie Miller began to emerge from all the shadows as a UCLA sophomore. Walt Hazzard replaced Larry Farmer as Bruins coach, and things began to turn around for Miller. The whole slumping Bruins basketball program also got a boost. The new coach liked Miller's style of play. With Miller bombing home points, the team finally caught fire late in the season. They won 13 of their last 19 games, and Reggie missed only 27 of 715 minutes in playing time during his team's final 17 games. Reggie Miller was also UCLA's leading scorer, the first sophomore to do this since Bill Walton a dozen seasons earlier.

The Bruins had something to prove when they returned to New York and Madison Square Garden at the end of the season to play in the National Invitational Tournament. Earlier in the year they had been embarrassed there by St. John's University in a game in which Miller had not played. It had been that humiliating loss that had convinced Coach Hazzard to give younger players like Reggie Miller a chance to play more regularly in the starting lineup.

The showdown game for the tournament championship matched UCLA with Indiana

# FACT

Only two UCLA Bruins have scored more career points than Reggie Miller has. Here's how Miller compares with other top scorers in UCLA basketball history:

| | SEASONS | POSITION | GAMES | POINTS | PPG |
|---|---|---|---|---|---|
| **Don MacLean** | 1989–1992 | Forward | 127 games | 2,608 points | 20.5 ppg. |
| **Lew Alcindor\*** | 1967–1969 | Center | 88 games | 2,325 points | 26.4 ppg. |
| **Reggie Miller** | 1984–1987 | Guard | 122 games | 2,095 points | 17.2 ppg. |
| **Ed O'Bannon** | 1992–1995 | Forward | 117 games | 1,815 points | 15.5 ppg. |
| **Tracy Murray** | 1990–1992 | Forward | 98 games | 1,792 points | 18.3 ppg. |
| **Bill Walton** | 1972–1974 | Center | 87 games | 1,767 points | 20.3 ppg. |

*\* Later changed name to Kareem Abdul-Jabbar*

University, coached by Bobby Knight and featuring its own sophomore star, Steve Alford. Alford was an excellent outside shooter like Reggie Miller. The two dueled head-to-head in the championship game. Indiana started fast and led most of the first half, but never by more than six points. It was a jump shot by Miller that tied the contest just before halftime. When Miller got hot early in the second half, the UCLA team took control of the game. With Miller and Alford both tossing in key baskets down the stretch, UCLA held on to win 65–62. Also close was the voting for tournament most valuable player. Reggie Miller captured the honor by a narrow margin over Steve Alford.

The tournament championship meant a moment of redemption for the basketball program at UCLA. It also meant redemption for the Bruins' latest star, Reggie Miller. Coach Hazzard spoke of what the moment meant. "A magazine article said Reggie couldn't beat his sister one-on-one," the coach recalled. "I wish the writer would put some salt and pepper on it and eat that article."[5] Miller also had words for the media about what he and his team had accomplished: "This is really sweet. We and the coach took a lot of verbal abuse."[6]

Miller was beginning to establish a solid reputation of his own. He was soon practicing with some of the stars of the NBA Los Angeles Lakers who often visited the campus for informal workouts in the Bruins gym. It was through encouragement from pros like Magic Johnson of the Lakers that Reggie began to realize the NBA might have a place in his own immediate future.

During his final two seasons with the Bruins, Miller became one of the nation's top scorers. He ranked fourth in the country as a junior with 26 points per game. In his senior season there was a

*While at UCLA, Reggie Miller tested his skills against Los Angeles Lakers players who came to the college for informal workouts. Now as a Pacer, he continues to vie with the Lakers on the NBA courts.*

new three-point rule that awarded an extra point for baskets made from farther than 19 feet 9 inches from the basket. It was the same rule that had long been used by the professionals to add excitement to their game. Using the new rule to his advantage, Miller climbed near the top of the list of UCLA's all-time greatest scorers. He hit nearly 45 percent of his three-point baskets and reached the 2,000 career point total as a senior. Only Lew Alcindor had previously scored that many points while playing at UCLA.

Cheryl Miller had been busy, too. She finished college with a long list of records, honors, and unmatched achievements. Reggie Miller was not yet a bigger star than his sister, but he was now ready for the NBA. Women did not yet have a popular professional league where they could continue to shine after college. For Reggie Miller, there was a new and grand stage awaiting. He was finally about to become the biggest star of the talented Miller clan.

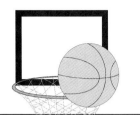

# Chapter 4

# Making It in the NBA

**B**oom Baby!" is a phrase familiar to every fan of the Indiana Pacers and every pro basketball fan in central Indiana. It is the "battle cry" called out excitedly by a popular Pacers radio broadcaster, and it has become a symbol of Indiana Pacers basketball in the 1990s. The phrase was invented by former Pacers coach Bob "Slick" Leonard, who has been a radio voice for the team for thirteen seasons.[1] It refers to the team's greatest offensive weapon, the bombs-away three-point shot by Reggie Miller. Leonard yells "Boom Baby!" into the radio microphone every time one of Miller's long-range missiles swishes through an empty basket. It has become a trademark not only of Miller's game, but of the Indiana Pacers team itself.

*As a rookie, Reggie Miller broke the record Larry Bird had previously set for three-point baskets.*

Reggie Miller was not always the most popular or most productive star. Miller was certainly not at first the kind of player who took the league by overnight storm. Playing in Indianapolis and not in the major media markets of Chicago, Los Angeles, or New York, it took time to capture the type of national attention lavished on players like Air Jordan and Scottie Pippen, or Shaquille O'Neal and Patrick Ewing. As a raw NBA rookie, Miller barely averaged double figures in scoring. But he did already display his talent as an outside bomber. And he played in every one of his team's eighty-two grueling games.

As a rookie in 1988, Reggie Miller had his lowest scoring season ever, yet still managed to set a new league record for three-point shooting by a first-year player, a record held at the time by the legendary Larry Bird of the Boston Celtics. He threw in 61 of his 172 shot attempts from beyond the "home run" circle—a line 23 feet 9 inches from the basket that separates two-point goals from three-point goals. It was an accuracy level of 35 percent, which was second best on the Indiana team. It was a mark that also bested Bird's first-year total for three-pointers by three baskets.

The 1990 season, his third, found Miller doing most of the scoring and most of the crowd pleasing. He posted the highest scoring average of his career, almost 25 points per game. Slowly but surely he climbed toward the top in the record books as Indiana's all-time greatest offensive player. Along the way he became the only NBA sharpshooter to lead his team in scoring during every season of the 1990s. This was something that even Michael Jordan, who retired for good in 1999, could not do. The string began when Miller took over the team's offensive burden from Chuck Person in the 1990 campaign and continued uninterrupted nine seasons later.

It was in his third season that Miller became a true star, averaging 20-plus points for the first time and becoming the Pacers' recognized offensive leader. For his improved play, Miller was named to the mid-season 1990 NBA All-Star Game roster. He was the first Indiana Pacer selected since way back in 1977, when Don Buse and Billy Knight had earned the only other selections in Pacers history.

The Pacers' new offensive star would also average 20 or more points for the next three seasons. Reggie Miller was now one of the league's most potent offensive players, though he never received much recognition among the league's designated superstars. Part of the reason was that he was not in New York, Chicago, or Los Angeles. And his team was not one of the league's elite teams.

## FACT

Some of Reggie Miller's individual game highs in the NBA are:

| | | |
|---|---|---|
| Points | 57 | at Charlotte, Nov. 28, 1992 |
| Field Goals Made | 16 | at Charlotte, Nov. 28, 1992 |
| Three-Point Field Goals Made | 8 | twice |
| Free Throws Made | 21 | at Charlotte, Nov. 28, 1992 |
| Rebounds | 12 | at Orlando, Dec. 18, 1996 |
| Assists | 11 | vs. Charlotte, Jan. 30, 1991 |
| Steals | 6 | vs. Sacramento, Feb. 17, 1993 |

Nevertheless, Miller stirred considerable notice. Finally, during the 1991 campaign, he stood among the elite offensive players in the NBA. That season—his fourth—Miller led the NBA in free-throw shooting, an area in which he would excel time and again in the future. His ability to get to the foul line, combined with his accuracy as a free-throw shooter, proved one of the enduring strengths of his game.

During the 1993 season, Reggie Miller continued his climb toward the top of the league's elite. For the second time, he was an NBA individual champion, now leading the circuit in three-point field goals—

just missing the existing NBA record by a mere five shots. Miller had the biggest night of his career early in the season when he caught fire in the Charlotte Coliseum against the Hornets and drilled 57 points.

Despite his displays of scoring, Reggie Miller was not yet in the category with Michael Jordan, Magic Johnson, or Larry Bird. He had only once been a league All-Star, and he had yet to be voted to the starting team for the prestigious midseason game. Nonetheless, he had made a start in his assault on true stardom. In Indianapolis, if nowhere else, Reggie Miller was well on his way to being one of basketball's biggest fan favorites.

Most young NBA players hope someday to be "big shots" by becoming recognized celebrities in the glamorous world of professional sports and television entertainment. However, the Indiana Pacers' biggest star was destined to become a "big shot" in a more literal sense. Reggie Miller was fast becoming known as one of basketball's greatest pure shooters and also as a player who could almost always be counted on to make the "big shot" whenever his team needed a crucial game-winning score.[2]

Miller can score from anywhere on the floor, and consistent scoring has always been the specialty that highlights his overall game. Many players can do many things on a basketball court with more flair

*Reggie Miller scores from any position—outside with a jumper or inside with a slam dunk.*

than Miller—showboat dribbling, hang-time leaping above the rim, pinpoint passing, and power-packed slam dunking. But when it comes to simply shooting the ball, there are few others in quite the same league with Reggie Miller—especially when the shooting is needed in the closing seconds of an important ballgame. In an age when slam dunking has become the most popular playground move, Miller is a throwback to earlier days, when players took greatest pride in their long-range bombing skills.

This ability to make important shots was never more apparent than at the end of the 1998 season, Miller's first year playing under new Pacers coach Larry Bird. Bird was himself one of the game's biggest clutch performers when he starred for the Boston Celtics. Coach Bird, as much as anyone, could appreciate Reggie Miller's ability to take over the final moments of any game single-handedly. "He amazes me," admitted Larry Bird, "and I've been around this league a long, long time."[3]

In little more than a month, between January 10 and February 19, Reggie Miller hit game-winning baskets in almost half of the Pacers' twenty-one games. First, he canned a three-pointer with only 32.5 seconds remaining in a game against Dallas. Another three-pointer beat Detroit four nights later.

*Reggie Miller was not an overnight sensation in the NBA but slowly emerged as the league's premiere practitioner of the ancient art of jump shooting.*

A third "home run"—what NBA players call the three-pointer—saved a Boston game during the final two minutes. And six more games were closed out with Miller's clutch shots in the final moments—often the final seconds—of game action. He missed a game-winner on the road at Orlando in late February. Yet only two nights later, he took control again when he dribbled around Philadelphia Sixers guard Eric Snow to drill a game-winning

## FACT

Reggie Miller is one of the best three-point shooters in NBA history. Here are some of his records and achievements in three-point shooting:

- Broke Larry Bird's rookie record for three-point field goals during 1988 season.
- Led NBA with 167 three-point field goals in 1993, missing league record by only five.
- Set playoff record for three-pointers made in a quarter with 5 at New York in 1994.
- Leading three-point shooter on 1996 Olympic "Dream Team III."
- One of only two players with six three-pointers in a half twice during playoffs.
- Passed Dale Ellis in 1998 as NBA career leader in three-point field goals with 1,596.

twenty-footer, delivering to his team an important road victory.

"Reggie wants to take the game-winner. He is not afraid of failing." This was the assessment back in 1996 of Herb Brown, a Pacers assistant coach and also the brother of Head Coach Larry Brown.[4] And Larry Brown held exactly the same opinion when he called his star player "the best pure shooter in basketball."[5]

"He makes the biggest shots more often than the rest of us," marveled veteran Chris Mullin, a long-time sharpshooter with the Golden State Warriors before being traded to Indiana. Mullin, too, is one of the league's most dependable clutch shooters. "We just kind of do our thing, and when it comes crunch time he takes over. It's incredible."[6]

Miller held a similar view about his taking the big shots when a game hangs in the balance.

> When the game is on the line and the fans, players and people at home watching on TV know you need a bucket and you have the ball in your hands . . . well, there's really not too much anyone can do about it. That's the mark of a clutch player. There's really no fear. I've always had the notion that you can't be scared of failure. Hey, it happens in everyday life. You just can't be afraid to fail.[7]

Reggie Miller has never been afraid to try.

Despite all the setbacks that marked his childhood and later years on the basketball court, Miller has rarely failed. Consequently, Reggie Miller—despite all the odds stacked against him—has become a true NBA superstar. And that is why in Indianapolis—even if not in Chicago or New York or Los Angeles—Miller is today the biggest basketball hero of them all.

# Chapter 5

# All-Star and Dream Teamer

**O**n February 12, 1995, Reggie Miller established an important milestone in his career and also in the history of his team. On that date, the up-and-coming NBA backcourt star became the first Indiana Pacer to make the starting lineup for an NBA All-Star Game. (Only two other Pacers had ever played in an NBA All-Star Game, and that had been more than a dozen long seasons in the past—and not as starters.)

The Phoenix All-Star Game appearance was the biggest highlight in Reggie Miller's athletic career, yet it would be only one in a series of special moments that finally brought Miller his desired measure of fame during the 1994, 1995, and 1996 basketball seasons.

Reggie Miller's first taste of All-Star Game action had come five years earlier, in 1990, when he had been selected as one of the Eastern Conference's bench players for the midseason classic. He played that year in Miami Arena on the home floor of the new Miami Heat expansion team. Miller was picked as one of the reserve guards for a powerful East All-Stars lineup coached by Detroit's Chuck Daly and featuring such superstars as Charles Barkley and Larry Bird at the forward positions, Patrick Ewing at center, and Michael Jordan and Isiah Thomas in the backcourt.

While Jordan and Bird's group was crushing the Western Conference team 130-113, Miller saw fourteen minutes of action, dished out 3 assists, and made 2 of the 3 shots he attempted. The single miss came on his only attempt at flinging up one of his familiar three-point bombs. It was not a performance that grabbed any headlines. Magic Johnson of the Lakers was the game's star and MVP. But for fans of the Indiana Pacers, it was a rare thrill to see one of their favorites running the court alongside legends like Jordan, Bird, and Magic during the league's once-a-year showcase game.

Also that same winter, Reggie Miller fired up his ongoing competition with the league's biggest star, Chicago's incomparable Michael Jordan. Miller had held his own against Jordan in the past, though Jordan always seemed to take the last bow. In one 1988 preseason game, Miller aggravated the veteran

*Reggie Miller gained new status when he was selected as a starter on the 1995 Eastern Conference All-Star squad.*

superstar with his bold "trash talk" and was burned by the scoring onslaught of an unstoppable Air Jordan during the fourth quarter. From that early experience. Miller learned he could not intimidate the best offensive player in the world. In turn, he was hardly intimidated himself. He would not back down from even the great Michael Jordan, and in coming seasons the two top shooting guards in the NBA would stage some remarkable head-on collisions.

One of the most memorable of these matchups came in Indianapolis in January 1990. The shoot-out that night began in the first quarter when both men began firing in their best outside jumpers with regularity. Jordan could not contain Miller who had 13 points before the quarter was over. But Jordan proved more than Miller could handle, as well, knocking down 9 points of his own. The teams were tied at 30 for the first quarter, and in the second quarter while Reggie Miller rested, the Pacers moved out to a 65–49 advantage.

Miller took control in the second half, with 12 more points in the third quarter and then his team's first 8 points of the final session. Jordan kept up an onslaught of his own and had 35 points—most of them against Miller—by the time the final horn sounded. While it was a typical brilliant performance by Michael Jordan, Reggie Miller had shone even brighter. He had drilled 44, his most ever at the time, and had done so against the best backcourt defender in the NBA. And the Pacers had won the game 120–113. Miller would long remember the game as one of the most special of his career. Beating Michael Jordan head-to-head was a rare occurrence to be savored by even the biggest stars in the league.

For their own parts, Miller and Jordan maintained their mutual respect for each other's talents and competitive natures. It was a respect that would lead to many more heated competitions in years to come.

While Reggie Miller held his own against Jordan in their individual head-to-head competitions, he and the Pacers, nonetheless, always played second fiddle to Michael Jordan and the Bulls throughout the seasons of the early 1990s. In 1991, 1992, and 1993 Chicago won three consecutive NBA championships. The Pacers meanwhile struggled just to become a respectable challenger; Indiana trailed Chicago by a wide margin each year in the NBA's Central Division. Jordan won five MVP trophies and was yearly the crown jewel of NBA All-Star teams. Michael Jordan also headlined for the 1992 Olympic "Dream Team" while Reggie Miller had to settle for far less celebrity as a hometown star in Indianapolis. When Jordan temporarily retired for the 1994 and

1995 seasons, Reggie Miller suddenly began to find a far larger place in the national spotlight.

Reggie Miller had been disappointed not to make the Americans' 1992 Olympic "Dream Team," which played for an Olympic gold medal in Barcelona, Spain.[1] Two summers later, with Jordan on the sideline and Isiah Thomas also newly retired, Miller had his chance to play with a second "Dream Team" selected to compete in the World Basketball Championships scheduled for Toronto, Canada. With

*In a one-on-one match on the court, Reggie Miller usually held his own against Michael Jordan, basketball's greatest offensive player.*

Bird, Magic, and Jordan now all retired, and Barkley slowed by injuries, this new Dream Team II was crowded with less-glamorous and younger faces from the NBA ranks. It featured not only Reggie Miller, but also new headline players like Alonzo Mourning, Shaquille O'Neal, Larry Johnson, and Shawn Kemp. When the team began practices in Chicago in July 1994, many wondered aloud who might win an imaginary matchup between the new Dream Team II and the more celebrated original Dream Team. Miller himself—never at a loss for words on or off the court—chimed in with an opinion also voiced by Shaquille O'Neal and Alonzo Mourning. It was Miller's view that this new Dream Team edition, with younger players and fresher legs, would have little trouble soundly beating its veteran forerunners.[2]

When competitions began in Toronto in August, there was no debate about how Dream Team II stacked up against current international opponents. The Americans seemed less than dominant in their opening 115–100 win over Spain. But they breezed through the next seven games. Reggie Miller—one of the Dream Team tricaptains—was labeled by one enthusiastic reporter as "the most compelling member" of the impressive Team USA squad. Miller was certainly one of the main contributors to an expected gold medal victory.[3] He was the team's

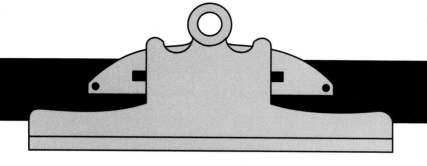

# STATS

Reggie Miller was a member of the "Dream Team III" that won an Olympic gold medal in Atlanta, Georgia. The other players on that "Dream Team" were

| NAME | POSITION | HEIGHT | NBA CLUB |
|------|----------|--------|----------|
| Charles Barkley | Forward | 6'6" | Phoenix Suns |
| Anfernee Hardaway | Guard | 6'7" | Orlando Magic |
| Grant Hill | Forward | 6'8" | Detroit Pistons |
| Karl Malone | Forward | 6'9" | Utah Jazz |
| Hakeem Olajuwon | Center | 7'0" | Houston Rockets |
| Shaquille O'Neal | Center | 7'1" | Orlando Magic |
| Gary Payton | Guard | 6'4" | Seattle SuperSonics |
| Scottie Pippen | Forward | 6'8" | Chicago Bulls |
| Mitch Richmond | Guard | 6'5" | Sacramento Kings |
| David Robinson | Center | 7'1" | San Antonio Spurs |
| John Stockton | Guard | 6'1" | Utah Jazz |

second-leading scorer, averaging 17 points. His 30 three-pointers were the most in the tournament. He canned a team-high 31 against Australia, and he made 8 of 11 three-point bombs versus Puerto Rico. With a combined 49 points in two halves of the games against Australia and Puerto Rico, the NBA's best long-range shooter made his lasting mark in the arena of international basketball competitions.

Recognition of Miller's new status also came with his selection as a 1995 NBA All-Star Game starter. An appearance in the showcase game in Phoenix was a milestone for both Reggie Miller and the Pacers franchise. But this was also a chance for Miller to demonstrate his extraordinary shooting talents for the wider television audience found in sections of the country where Pacers games were not often broadcast. It, of course, helped Miller and other attention-seeking younger stars that Michael Jordan was not around at All-Star time for a second straight year. (He retired briefly, to try his hand at baseball, before returning to the NBA.) Sacramento's Mitch Richmond—not Reggie Miller—stole the spotlight as the surprise Most Valuable Player and the Western Conference team ran to an easy 139–112 victory. But Miller made as much of a splash and as much history as anyone cared about back home in Indiana when he lined up alongside Shaquille O'Neal, Grant Hill, Penny Hardaway, and Scottie Pippen in the Eastern Conference starting lineup.

A year later the greatest honor of all came to Reggie Miller when it was announced he had gained a coveted place on still another All-Star squad, Dream

## FACT

Reggie Miller was the first Indiana Pacer selected as an All-Star Game starter (in 1995) and also the only Pacer to make more than one NBA All-Star team. Here are the Pacers who have played in NBA All-Star Games:

| PLAYER | YEAR | POSITION | TEAM | GAME PERFORMANCE |
|---|---|---|---|---|
| Don Buse | 1977 | Guard | West | Substitute 19 minutes, 4 points |
| Billy Knight | 1977 | Forward | West | Substitute 12 minutes, 4 points |
| Reggie Miller | 1990 | Guard | East | Substitute 14 minutes, 4 points |
| Detlef Schrempf | 1993 | Forward | East | Substitute 13 minutes, 3 points |
| Reggie Miller | 1995 | Guard | East | Starter 23 minutes, 9 points |
| Reggie Miller | 1996 | Guard | East | Substitute 18 minutes, 8 points |
| Reggie Miller | 1998 | Guard | East | Substitute 20 minutes, 14 points |
| Rik Smits | 1998 | Center | East | Substitute 21 minutes, 10 points |

Team III, the roster of NBA superstars chosen to represent America during 1996 Summer Olympic competitions. Miller again did far more than merely make a token appearance on the gold-medal-winning team that dominated basketball play in Atlanta. He was the team's leader in three-point shooting. He was also the Team USA pacesetter in the number of total minutes played. Surrounded by future Hall-of-Famers like Hakeem Olajuwon, Shaquille O'Neal, John Stockton, Karl Malone, and Charles Barkley, it was Miller who saw more action than any other Team

USA player. He averaged more than 21 minutes on the floor during each Olympic contest.

Dream Team III, like its forerunners, again handily beat all of its opposition. But it was not always easy. This time the average margin of victory was merely 33 points per game. Dream Team III opened its eight-game stroll to still another American gold medal with a 96–68 thumping of Argentina. The gold medal was won as expected two weeks later in a one-sided match with Croatia (formerly part of Yugoslavia)—a team with a couple of NBA players of its own named Vlade Divac (Charlotte Hornets) and Sasha Davilovic (Miami Heat). Reggie Miller saved his biggest scoring outburst of 20 points for the final game of the tournament, raising his Olympic average to 11.4 points per game. Playing in the company of so many great professional and international stars, Miller had quite adequately met the toughest challenge of his basketball career. But Reggie Miller was not satisfied.

"Until I get to the Finals and have a shot at winning a championship ring, it's not ever over. I've got to get to the Finals. I've got to perform in the Finals, where everything is truly on the line."[4] It was not the trophies or scoring records or gold medals that Reggie Miller cherished. It was this burning desire to win an NBA team title that already made Reggie Miller a true NBA champion.

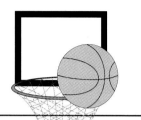

# Chapter 6

# NBA Superstar

**R**eggie Miller built on his Dream Team experiences to launch one of his most successful NBA campaigns. The 1995 season saw both Miller and the Pacers take up where they left off in the postseason campaign of 1994. Ironically, these were the only two seasons of the 1990s when Miller did not average above 20 points scoring for the regular season. They were also the two seasons when the Indiana team gelled under new head coach Larry Brown. For two years in a row, the Pacers set team records for winning, and both seasons they would fight their way into the conference postseason championship round. With Reggie Miller leading the way, the 1995 Pacers were, for the first and only time, the regular-season champions of the NBA Central Division.

The earlier campaign of 1994 was also a season of special highlights for Miller. He finished the season as one of two players in the league to shoot more than 90 percent from the free-throw line. He registered his ten-thousandth career point against the Bulls in January. His streak of consecutive games played also reached 345—the longest active streak in the league at that time—before he had to sit out a game against Houston on November 18 because of a sprained ankle.

The remarkable 1995 season would be topped off on June 1 with one of the greatest single performances in NBA playoff history. It all came about in a game that the Pacers simply had to win in order to remain alive in the crucial series that would determine the NBA's Eastern Conference champion. A New York victory would leave the Knicks only a single win short of the conference title with still one game remaining on their home floor of Madison Square Garden. And a Knicks victory looked pretty certain with the home team leading 70–58 at the end of three quarters and the Pacers' top offensive weapon, Miller, struggling with only six baskets for the entire night.

When there were a dozen minutes of action

*Reggie Miller has made a habit of shooting down Patrick Ewing and the New York Knicks during crucial playoff games for the NBA Eastern Conference Championship.*

remaining in the final quarter, Reggie Miller put on a display of scoring that confirmed for everyone how he was obviously the league's top performer when it came to the art of clutch, pressure-packed jump shooting.[1]

Reggie Miller's incredible onslaught began with a long three-point bomb in the opening seconds from behind a screen set by teammate Kenny Williams. For the next ten minutes Miller was truly "in a zone" as he rained jumpers from both sides of the court, missing on only two of his ten distant bombs. Except for four free throws and one fifteen-foot field goal, none of Miller's shots came from closer than nineteen feet. His 25 fourth-quarter points and 5 final-period three-point baskets were both playoff records. And more important, his one-man offensive explosion had left the stunned New York team reeling and had lifted the Pacers to a remarkable come-from-behind 93–86 victory.

Miller's theatrics that night were not limited to his net-burning shots—shots that came off the dribble, from behind screens, in the middle of defensive traffic, or far outside the three-point line and away from Knicks defenders. Knicks superfan Spike Lee was in his usual seat at courtside. Lee had taunted Reggie earlier in the game when Miller's shots were all missing badly. It was now time for

Miller to return the trash talk, and after several of his fourth-quarter bombs, Miller turned to face Lee and stare down the famous film director, making an unmistakable gesture of hands around the throat that said, "The Knicks are choking!" Reggie Miller's 39 points and the Pacers' dramatic comeback were more than enough to add an exclamation point to Miller's return taunts.

The Pacers were making their first serious run that June at an NBA postseason title. Miller's fabulous performance put the Pacers in a position to win a conference championship on their home floor. But in the end they lost two dramatic final games in the Eastern Conference Finals against the arch rival New York Knicks. Both games were close at the end. In both games the Pacers had completely run out of last-minute heroics.

All in all, things were now looking up in Indiana, after two painful decades as a lackluster NBA franchise. If the Pacers in the end fell short against Ewing and the Knicks, there would be an encore performance only a single season later. It came in another Eastern Conference Championship matchup, this time with the Orlando Magic and their young superman center, Shaquille O'Neal. Orlando would also knock Reggie Miller's Pacers from the championship round, just as Ewing and the

Knicks had done one summer earlier, but not before Miller stole a piece of center stage during NBA playoff crunch time.

Before the Pacers could get to the Magic and their Shaquille O'Neal-led "Shaq Attack" there was

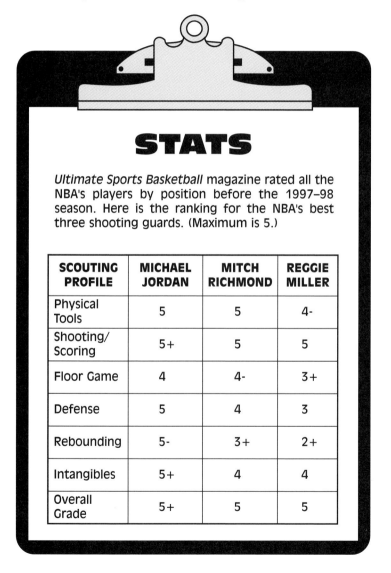

# STATS

*Ultimate Sports Basketball* magazine rated all the NBA's players by position before the 1997–98 season. Here is the ranking for the NBA's best three shooting guards. (Maximum is 5.)

| SCOUTING PROFILE | MICHAEL JORDAN | MITCH RICHMOND | REGGIE MILLER |
|---|---|---|---|
| Physical Tools | 5 | 5 | 4- |
| Shooting/ Scoring | 5+ | 5 | 5 |
| Floor Game | 4 | 4- | 3+ |
| Defense | 5 | 4 | 3 |
| Rebounding | 5- | 3+ | 2+ |
| Intangibles | 5+ | 4 | 4 |
| Overall Grade | 5+ | 5 | 5 |

another postseason showdown with the Knicks and their Reggie Miller nemesis superfan, Spike Lee. Again, Madison Square Garden was turned into a special Reggie Miller showplace. The following Pacers-Knicks shoot-out proved to be one of the highlights of the entire NBA season.

Game 5 against the Knicks in New York a year earlier had brought one of the best individual performances in league history from Miller. This new postseason matchup with New York produced a near repeat effort from Indiana's most famous bomber. Game 1 of the Eastern Conference semifinals opened in Madison Square Garden on May 7. This time Miller keyed one of the most remarkable comebacks in playoff annals. He somehow scored 8 points in just 8.9 seconds of the game's final half-minute to lift the Pacers to an important opening-night win. With playoff pride squarely on the line, Miller had driven a dagger into the New York Knicks. He stunned both the New York players and the partisan Madison Square Garden crowd, as well as a national audience of disbelieving television viewers.

Reggie Miller always enjoyed challenges, and the challenge he faced in Madison Square Garden on May 7, 1995, was one of his biggest. The Pacers were trailing the Knicks by six points, 105–99, with only eighteen ticks remaining on the scoreboard clock. It was the important opening game of the playoff second round, and a Knicks victory would give the rivals a huge advantage. But if Indiana fans, and perhaps even the Indiana players, had given the game up as lost, Reggie Miller certainly had not.

For most of the game, Miller struggled. His outside shot was off target most of the time, and he had connected on only 7 of his 18 shots. It was seven-foot-four center Rik Smits who had carried the Pacers all evening, before fouling out with 1:40 remaining. Smits seemed the best player on the floor that night. He scored a playoff career-high 34 and held Knicks' star center, Patrick Ewing, to only 11. When Smits drew his sixth personal foul, however, Indiana's chances seemed to fly out the window. "We were pretty down," Smits recalled after the game. "But it's never over till it's over. I've seen weirder things happen."[2] What happened next was so weird, however, that even the most optimistic Pacers fan could not have dreamed it up.

Miller, of course, knew the odds were stacked against his team once Rik Smits went to the bench. "When you're down by six with fifteen, twenty seconds left, it doesn't look good. But you can never give up."[3] But Miller had already proven time and again that he never gave up, especially when faced

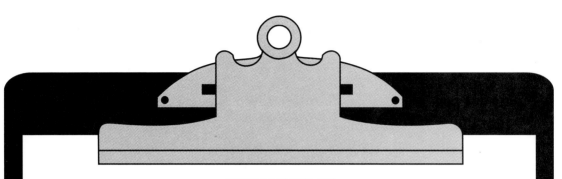

# STATS

Only five players in NBA history have made better than 50 percent of their field-goal shots and also better than 90 percent of their free-throw shots during the same season. Reggie Miller and Indiana Pacers coach Larry Bird are the only players to accomplish such expert shooting twice.

| PLAYER | TEAM | SEASON | FG% | FT% |
|--------|------|--------|-----|-----|
| Reggie Miller | Indiana Pacers | 1993–94 | .503 | .908 |
| Reggie Miller | Indiana Pacers | 1990–91 | .512 | .918 |
| Jeff Malone | Utah Jazz | 1990–91 | .508 | .917 |
| Mark Price | Cleveland Cavs | 1988–89 | .526 | .901 |
| Magic Johnson | Los Angeles Lakers | 1988–89 | .509 | .911 |
| Larry Bird | Boston Celtics | 1987–88 | .527 | .916 |
| Larry Bird | Boston Celtics | 1986–87 | .525 | .910 |

with impossible odds. The exit of Rik Smits from the floor meant that it was time for Reggie Miller to take over the game and rescue the Pacers with his incredible shooting skills and coolness in the heat of battle.

The memorable nine seconds of Miller's heroics turned out to be one of the NBA's most unforgettable highlight sequences. Miller first drilled a dramatic three-pointer to cut the Knicks' lead to 105–102. Then he immediately stole the inbounds pass thrown carelessly by New York's Anthony Mason, calmly dashed behind the three-point line, and canned another three-point goal, which tied the score. It had all happened in just 3.1 seconds. The Knicks were so shaken that next John Starks missed badly on two free throws, and Ewing did not make a ten-footer he put up with 9.9 seconds remaining. The partisan crowd and the disorganized Knicks—as well as the nationwide television audience—were completely stunned by the time Miller was fouled two seconds later and calmly canned the final two free throws to clinch the improbable 107–105 Indiana victory.

Pacers coach Larry Brown could hardly believe what he had just seen unfold. In the postgame press conference, Brown admitted he was "in a state of disbelief because I never imagined that one. . . . I can't remember something like that."[4]

*In Game 3 of the 1995 playoff series, the Pacers defeated the Knicks thanks to Reggie Miller's sensational last-minute clutch shooting.*

Miller kept up his postseason shooting onslaught against the Orlando Magic during the Eastern Conference Finals. His 25 three-point goals in seven games was second all time in league history, trailing only the 28 that Orlando's Dennis Scott threw down during the very same series.

Again, the Pacers came close to reaching the NBA's final championship round, just as they had a year earlier. Game 4 of the Eastern Conference Finals saw the same kind of late-game Indiana heroics the Pacers and Reggie Miller were rapidly becoming famous for. The setting was the home floor at Market Square Arena. This time, the Pacers would be saved not by Reggie Miller but by Rik Smits. Smits drilled a last-second shot that capped the game's storybook finish. It was one of the wildest finishes in NBA history, with Scott, Miller and Orlando's Penny Hardaway all canning three-pointers during the final 13 seconds.

Smits was the hero of the last-second win that kept the Pacers alive. Trailing by one point with 1.3 seconds on the clock, the Pacers inbounded to Smits who leaned around Magic center Tree Rollins for the remarkable game winner. Miller had played a huge role as well. Throughout the game, he supplied most of the firepower. In the wild closing seconds Miller had supplied a big three-point shot with 5 seconds left that had put the Pacers in a position to win.

*During the 1995 Eastern Conference Championship series, Reggie Miller continued his great postseason performance against Shaquille O'Neal and Penny Hardaway of the Orlando Magic.*

Two games later, Miller once more supplied much of the offense as the Pacers romped home in a victory that set up a deciding Eastern Conference Championship game. He simply tore up the Magic with his deadly shooting in the first half. He had 20 in the first quarter and 28 at the intermission as the Pacers built an insurmountable 25-point margin and never looked back. It may have been Miller's finest hour among so many fine hours for the Indiana Pacers incomparable star shooter.

The Magic had the home court advantage in this series. In the end the scales again tipped away from the Pacers and toward their opponents. In Game 7, back in Orlando, the Pacers were never really in the game during a lopsided 105–81 blowout. For Reggie Miller, it was a most disappointing moment, to come ever so close and yet again fail to make it into the final series and the final battle for an NBA championship.[5] For two years in a row, Miller and the Pacers had come within earshot of their ultimate goal. The team would now have to begin building all over again and wait patiently for another season to unfold.

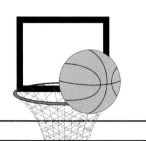

# Chapter 7

# Shooting in the Shadows

**R**eggie Miller is one star athlete who seems to have it all—a multimillion-dollar contract, a reputation as one of basketball's most talented long-range, three-point bombers, a successful marriage with fashion model Marita Starvou-Miller, and an adoring public in one of the NBA's most fan-crazed cities of Indianapolis. Despite this appearance of endless success, one of pro basketball's most popular players has had to struggle with huge challenges, many disappointments, and a negative public image that has sometimes clouded his achievements.

Even Miller's status as the most talented and popular player in Indiana Pacers history often takes a backseat to his widespread image as one of basketball's most colorful "bad boys." Many see Miller only as a "trash talking showboat," best known for "loose cannon" behavior and comments to the press, a flamboyant personality, and brazen self-confidence. When Miller almost single-handedly carried his Pacers into the 1994 NBA Finals, his scoring outburst against the New York Knicks seemed to take a backseat to his outspoken postgame press conferences and his personal "war of words" with Knicks superfan Spike Lee. Teammate Byron Scott was once quick to point out that Miller's reputation for trash talking has made him "the most hated man" in the eyes of most NBA opponents and fans.[1]

A "trash talker" is a player who annoys opponents with constant taunting. Reggie explained that most of this behavior was simply to psyche himself up on the court. (It is widely reported that his behavior off the court is drastically different. He gives much of his time and money to help others.[2]) Others saw it differently. He was a player that got under other players' skins. And he incited rival crowds as well.

It was a role Miller relished. He would explain this in his book (written with sportswriter Gene Wojciechowski), which was appropriately titled

## FACT

A "trash talker" is a player who verbally insults his oppo-
nent during the heat of play in order to rattle and
distract him. Here is a list of some of pro basketball's
most notorious current trash talkers:

| PLAYER | POSITION | NBA TEAM |
| --- | --- | --- |
| Reggie Miller | Guard | Indiana Pacers |
| Charles Barkley | Forward | Houston Rockets |
| John Starks | Guard | Golden State Warriors |
| Allen Iverson | Guard | Philadelphia Sixers |

*I Love Being the Enemy*.[3] But it also was a trait that
sometimes tarnished his image. Reggie Miller was
as famous around the league and to millions of television basketball viewers for his brash trash talking
and outspoken boasts as he was for his many displays
of clutch shooting.

Miller has always been determined to overcome
any obstacles in his path and to battle for his own
starring role in the game at which he excels. After
the Indiana Pacers' near-miss seasons of 1994 and
1995, Reggie Miller was at long last a genuine NBA

*Reggie Miller is one of the most sensational and unguardable shooting guards in the NBA today.*

star in his own right. He was also the toast of the town throughout Indianapolis. He was equally loved elsewhere as a champion of all those who hated the dominance of teams from New York.[4]

There had been rumors for several seasons that Miller might sign a contract in another city when he became a free agent at the end of his current contract. Perhaps he would end up in New York, where he had such a knack for heroics in Madison Square Garden. Or perhaps the lure of the bright lights in his hometown of Los Angeles would beckon. Such speculations were sometimes a distraction throughout the 1996 basketball season, a year that saw the Pacers struggle to maintain their newfound position among the league's elite teams.

In the end, Reggie Miller signed once more with the Pacers, something that he had always wanted to do. His new four-year contract was for almost $40 million, or $10 million a year. That made him one of the wealthiest athletes in the land. Miller took special pride in playing with a single team and remaining in a town that had always treated him as its top sports hero.

Miller explained his choice in these terms. "A lot of kids have grown up watching Reggie Miller and identify with me. To me, one of the things that has hurt sports the most is the kids seeing these guys moving around. Coming in and playing in one place your whole career stands for something."[5]

Indiana matched its record of 52 wins during its third season under Larry Brown. But the team nonetheless slid behind Chicago in the Central Division standings. Jordan was back on his game in Chicago, and the Bulls, not surprisingly, raced to the best season in league history, leaving the Pacers and everyone else in the dust.

It was a year that was also plagued with misfortune and injury for the entire Pacers team. Center Rik Smits missed nineteen games and was troubled by an ankle injury that eventually needed season-ending surgery. And there was Miller's severe eye injury just before season's end. It spelled doom for the star-crossed Pacers during the playoffs.

Indiana did not hang around long in their third trip to the year-end playoffs under Larry Brown. Atlanta made short work of an Indiana team that was not at full strength. Many in Indianapolis felt that the team that was so good only a year earlier should never have lost to Atlanta, even without Miller in the lineup and the team not at full strength. The Pacers and their storybook ride under Coach Larry Brown seemed to be unraveling.

The slide that began in 1996 became a runaway

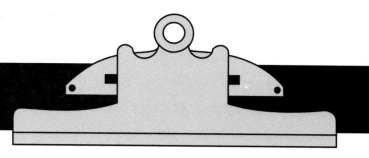

# STATS

Reggie Miller's greatest pride comes from playing his whole career with a single NBA team, something few current stars have done. Here is a list of seven current NBA veterans with at least ten years' experience who have played their entire careers with only one team (as of 1998).

| PLAYER | ROOKIE YEAR | TEAM | SEASONS |
|---|---|---|---|
| Hakeem Olajuwon | 1984–85 | Houston Rockets | 14 |
| John Stockton | 1984–85 | Utah Jazz | 14 |
| Karl Malone | 1985–86 | Utah Jazz | 13 |
| Joe Dumars | 1985–86 | Detroit Pistons | 13 |
| Patrick Ewing | 1985–86 | New York Knicks | 13 |
| Nate McMillan | 1986–87 | Seattle SuperSonics | 12 |
| Reggie Miller | 1987–88 | Indiana Pacers | 11 |

downhill snowball a year later. Smits was out for the first third of the 1997 season after surgery to his troublesome feet. Once Smits was back, another key performer was lost when defensive star forward Derrick McKey went to the injured list.

Miller continued his scoring onslaughts and his on-floor leadership. But the team under fourth-year coach Larry Brown was now a rapidly sinking ship. Brown was an intense coach with a reputation for first firing up teams but then burning out his players. The result was a losing season and a place on the sidelines when playoff time rolled around. The Pacers' 39 victories were the fewest in eight seasons. The team record had fallen below .500 for the first season in five years. For the first time in the 1990s, there would be no playoffs in Indianapolis. This was from a team that two years earlier seemed the heir-apparent to Michael Jordan's Chicago Bulls. The season had been nothing short of a full-scale disaster.

No one was happy in Indiana by year's end—at least not among those who worked or played for the Indiana Pacers or among the dedicated fans who followed the team's fortunes. Shortly after the season ended, Larry Brown decided to pull out and try his luck with a new team in Philadelphia. Brown was still a highly respected coach everywhere

*Being the enemy and charging up the fans in opposing cities is a role that Reggie Miller truly loves to play.*

around the league, and he was quickly offered a multimillion-dollar contract to rebuild the fortunes of the struggling Philadelphia Sixers team. Back in Indiana they would be searching for a replacement who could fill coach Brown's shoes and start the team going in the right direction again.

Even Reggie Miller was now considering whether or not it might be time to end his own career in Indiana. He had played well enough in his tenth season, but the passion was gone from the team. In the burned-out wreck of the Pacers' disappointing season, the passion seemed to be gone from the star player as well.

Pacers management knew from the start who they wanted to occupy Coach Brown's role. It had been a rumor for a year or two that Larry Bird—the greatest of all Indiana basketball legends—might be ready to end his five-year retirement and rejoin the game. Bird wanted to coach, but not in Boston where he had been a star player. The Boston team had been slumping for several years, and the lack of talent there meant Bird could never meet expectations in a town where he was an unmatched legend. His home state of Indiana might just be the answer. At least that is what Pacers general manager Donnie Walsh hoped.

It seemed a match made in basketball heaven.

Bird would need a veteran team to coach, one with veteran players who were mature enough to benefit from his laid-back approach. The Pacers franchise needed a coach who would merit immediate respect and who would not micromanage. That meant a coach who would not try to design every play and reteach veteran stars things they already knew.[6]

The Pacers could not resist Bird, and Bird could not resist the Pacers. Larry Bird announced in May that he would return to Indiana and take up coaching. The Pacers' head coaching problem was solved. The only shadow on the horizon for the Pacers was the low spirits of their superstar, Reggie Miller. Miller could benefit more than anyone else perhaps from a coach like Larry Bird. If Bird was to be successful in coaching the Pacers, he would need a star like Miller to carry the team's offense. Just about everyone in Indiana knew this. It was fondly hoped by the Pacers management and the Indianapolis fans that Reggie Miller knew it, too.

# Chapter 8

# A Legend Playing for a Legend

**B**efore it was over, the new basketball season that began in November 1996 would provide some of Reggie Miller's most disheartening moments as a professional athlete. First, the Indiana Pacers unexpectedly slid from playoff prominence as one of the league's elite teams. Miller himself performed poorly—at least by his own standards—after signing a new four-year, $36-million contract with the team. And the brief four-year era of Coach Larry Brown came to a most disappointing end in Indianapolis.

There was also personal tragedy for Miller and his wife as their new multimillion-dollar dream home in Indianapolis was burned to the ground as a result of a fire that someone intentionally set. The police have never been able to identify and arrest the criminals who performed the vicious act of setting fire to the Millers' house. Reggie Miller has remained fearful that someone may still be out there following his every move and intending to harm him further.[1] As always, Miller would quickly rebound from his personal adversities, and eventually his team would rebound along with him.

Miller had been so disappointed by the previous year, especially by the act of arson that had destroyed his home, that he was beginning to wonder whether he still wanted to play for the Pacers—or whether he wanted to play basketball at all. If Bird had not arrived on the scene, Miller probably would have left. But Bird was able to help the disillusioned player put everything in perspective.

Bird told Miller that things like the vicious fire that destroyed his home sometimes happen when an athlete or celebrity is in the public eye. There are always jealous people, Bird cautioned, and you have to accept this fact and move on. The former great player told Reggie Miller that this was still Miller's team and his town. He simply could not let a single bad apple spoil everything.[2] Besides, the new coach and Miller's old teammates needed their superstar more than ever.

*Personal loss and disappointment in 1997 almost ended his career, but Reggie Miller would soon rebound to enjoy his most satisfying season ever.*

The message and its timing were perfect. "That made me feel good, that he believed so much in me," Miller told Indianapolis sportswriter Mark Montieth.[3] Reggie Miller realized that this could be a very special season with Larry Bird. Perhaps the dream of winning an NBA championship could be rekindled, and that would be enough to wipe from memory any team and personal losses of the past two years.

While he waited for the 1997–98 season to open, Reggie Miller tried his hand at a new off-court career. Again following a trail blazed by his talented sister, Miller became a commentator for televised games of the Women's National Basketball Association (WNBA), the new women's pro league.

"The idea of showing these athletes as heroes and role models for young women was what really persuaded me to be part of the coverage," revealed Miller. "But it does feel weird to be on the other side of the fence. I'm a member of the media now."[4]

The haunting memories of the fire would not leave immediately, even after the new season started. Reggie Miller became more cautious in public. He hired security and was not so open with his many fans. He wondered whether the person who set fire to his house might even be coming to Market Square Arena to watch him play.[5] If

# FACT

Reggie Miller has played for nine different head coaches in college and the NBA. Here is a list of coaches that Miller has played for:

| COACH | YEARS | TEAM | GAMES |
|-------|-------|------|-------|
| Larry Farmer | 1983–1984 | UCLA | 28 |
| Walt Hazzard | 1984–1987 | UCLA | 94 |
| Jack Ramsay | 1987–1988 | Indiana Pacers | 89 |
| Mel Daniels | 1988 | Indiana Pacers | 2 |
| George Irvine | 1988 | Indiana Pacers | 18 |
| Dick Versace | 1989–1990 | Indiana Pacers | 154 |
| Bob Hill | 1991–1993 | Indiana Pacers | 221 |
| Larry Brown | 1993–1997 | Indiana Pacers | 317 |
| Larry Bird | 1997–1998 | Indiana Pacers | 81 |

memories of the fire influenced Miller's public behavior, they certainly did not bother his play once basketball started again.

Reggie Miller was happy to be playing for Larry Bird, and Bird was happy to still have Miller in the fold. The Pacers fans shared that enthusiasm. Miller would now be playing with a coach he could fully respect like no other coach he had ever had. He was looking forward to a full season with a point guard and teammate who was one of his best friends.

Mark Jackson had been traded away the previous season and then rejoined the club late in the year. Now he would share the backcourt with Reggie Miller for a full season. But it was Larry Bird who provided the biggest lift.

"I'm very excited to be playing for a living legend," Miller told the press. "It's something this team really needed after the disappointing season we had. This is one guy who can come in here and put us back where we belong, in the upper elite. He was a fantastic player, I'm sure he'll be a fantastic coach."[6] In another interview Miller remarked that he felt "like a kid in a candy store. There are things I haven't had the opportunity to see that he's seen. Remember, he's seen everything."[7]

The Pacers started slowly under their new coach, losing five of their first seven games. But the downslide lasted only a few weeks. Before the season was only a month old, Bird had seemed to transform the Pacers into the same threat to the Bulls and the league's other teams that they had been a couple of years earlier.

It was clear from the start that Coach Bird had a different approach to the game from his predecessor Larry Brown. It was also different from most other NBA and college coaches. Larry Bird was a hands-off coach. He believed in preparing the players in practice but letting them control the action once a game began.

Bird's formula was simple enough. "I'm not a screamer. My whole thing is preparedness. We work these guys in practice. But I feel that once the game starts, let the players play the game. If a coach talks too much once the game starts, they don't listen."[8]

The Pacers remained on a roll throughout the entire season. By year's end they would have the best team record in franchise history. They finished the campaign with one of the best final months ever witnessed in Indianapolis. Bird also had his team prepared for the challenge when the NBA began its second season. (The second season is what the NBA playoffs are often called.) And the Indiana team was ready for that season as one of the strongest challengers for an elusive NBA championship.

It was also a rebound season for Reggie Miller. He continued his impressive string as the team's leading scorer. He regained the lead from Dale Ellis as the league's all-time three-point marksman. He moved into second place behind Mark Price among active players in free-throw accuracy. And in his eleventh season, he continued the same kind of statistical numbers that kept him near the top of the league's best performers. There were nearly 20 points a game. His shooting percentage was only a

*Indiana fans supported hometown basketball hero Larry Bird, even when he played for the Boston Celtics. In the summer of '97, fans were delighted when Bird returned home to coach the Pacers.*

# STATS

Reggie Miller seems to perform better under the pressure of the year-end playoffs. Here is a comparison of some of Miller's playoff and regular-season offensive stats through the 1998 season:

| STATISTICAL CATEGORY | PLAYOFFS | REGULAR SEASON |
|---|---|---|
| Scoring Average | 24.7 | 19.7 |
| FG Percentage | .481 | .485 |
| 3-Point FG Percentage | .436 | .401 |
| Free Throw Percentage | .861 | .877 |
| Rebounding Average | 3.2 | 3.2 |
| Assists Per Game | 2.6 | 3.1 |

fraction below 50 percent. He had a three-point shooting accuracy around 40 percent and a free-throw accuracy just under 90 percent. He produced the type of season that clearly demonstrated he was still near the top of his game.

Miller also got plenty of help. Rik Smits was back from a disappointing 1997 campaign of his own. Smits even made his first All-Star Game appearance. Dale Davis and Antonio Davis supplemented Smits under the basket and gave the Pacers one of the best front courts anywhere in the league. And Mark Jackson was again as good as any other guard in the league at running an offense and assisting scorers like Rik Smits and Reggie Miller.

By increasing his own already impressive statistics and earning still more spots in the NBA record book, Reggie Miller had more than likely taken another giant step toward joining sister Cheryl in basketball's Hall of Fame. But it was certainly not the records or personal acknowledgments that now inspired Miller as he approached the twilight years of his career.

Reggie Miller was still taking the floor every night throughout the 1998 season with the same two quarters from high school days taped under his wristband and his father's statement of years ago still ringing clearly in his ears. "No matter how many points you score, none of it's worth fifty cents unless you get that ring." Although Miller is quick to point to another brilliant year for himself and the Indiana Pacers, the NBA championship ring is still everything.[9] That ring is what true champions like Reggie Miller play for.

As the 1998 playoffs opened, the Pacers were perhaps the only serious threat in the Eastern Conference to end the three-year domination by the Chicago Bulls. Under the coaching of Larry Bird,

Reggie Miller was closer than ever to the one trophy that had long escaped him, an NBA Championship ring. The Pacers swept by the Cleveland Cavaliers and New York Knicks in early playoff rounds. Reggie Miller's last-minute heroics, especially against the Knicks, lifted Indiana once more into the Eastern Conference Finals. In crucial Game 4 of the New York series, it was the famed Knicks-killer who silenced Spike Lee and the Madison Square Garden faithful with a last-second display of heroic shooting. A three-point bomb by Miller with 1.5 seconds remaining allowed the Pacers to tie a game they would win in overtime. Indiana had the momentum needed to capture the do-or-die series.

This time the Pacers would battle the defending champion Chicago Bulls and superstar Michael Jordan, playing his final season, for a conference championship, and also for the right to finally advance into the NBA Finals against the Western Conference champions from Utah. In the end, the Pacers would again lose a seven-game series, just as they had in 1994 and 1995. Once more, Reggie Miller's championship dream was placed on hold, despite his own strong efforts, which included another miraculous last-second shot to win a pivotal fourth game in the series.

Gannett News Service sports columnist Mike

Lopresti put it best when he commented on the years of frustration that have kept Reggie Miller and the Pacers out of the season's final playoff round. Lopresti wrote a column suggesting that it would be just for the basketball gods to make room in the NBA Finals some year for Reggie Miller. "No man should play as well as he has in so many months of May," wrote Lopresti, "and yet never get the chance to play in June."[10]

*The Pacers' all-time leader in almost every category, Reggie Miller performs at his best during the pressures of postseason playoffs.*

# Chapter Notes

## Chapter 1. Reggie, Reggie!

1. Tom Reitmann, "Eye Injury Will Keep Miller Out Three Weeks," *Indianapolis Star/News*, April 15, 1996, p. 1.

2. Hank Hersch, "The Shape of Things to Come," *Sports Illustrated*, November 11, 1991, p. 132.

3. Mark Montieth, "Shoot to Thrill," *MVP Pro Basketball '98* (Lombard, Ill.: MVP Media, 1998), p. 16.

4. Ibid., p. 14.

## Chapter 2. Beaten by Your Big Sister

1. Hank Hersch, "The Shape of Things to Come," *Sports Illustrated*, November 11, 1991, p. 134.

2. Reggie Miller (with Gene Wojciechowski), *I Love Being the Enemy* (New York: Simon & Schuster, 1995), p. 45.

3. Ibid., pp. 46–47.

4. Ibid., p. 49.

5. "Lookout," *People*, December 12, 1983, p. 170.

6. Miller, p. 48.

7. "Welcome to Miller Time," *Sport*, April 1984, p. 16.

## Chapter 3. Just Another UCLA Bruins Legend

1. Reggie Miller (with Gene Wojciechowski), *I Love Being the Enemy* (New York: Simon & Schuster, 1995), p. 48.

2. Ibid.

3. Ibid., p. 47.

4. "Welcome to Miller Time," *Sport*, April 1984, p. 16.

5. Stew Thornley, *Sports Great Reggie Miller* (Springfield, N.J.: Enslow Publishers, Inc., 1996), p. 31.

6. Ibid.

## Chapter 4. Making It in the NBA

1. Conrad Brunner, *Boom Baby! The Sudden, Surprising Rise of the Indiana Pacers* (Indianapolis: Masters Press, 1994) p.iii

2. Kerry Eggars, "Pure and Simple, Miller Is a Big Shot," *The Oregonian*, March 10, 1996, p. 1.

3. Mark Montieth, "Shoot to Thrill," *MVP Pro Basketball '98* (Lombard, Ill.: MVP Media, 1998), p. 17.

4. Eggars, p. 1.

5. Ibid.

6. Montieth, p. 17.

7. David Benner, (ed.), *1997–98 Official Indiana Pacers Team Yearbook* (New York: Finlay Sports, 1998), p. 40.

## Chapter 5. All-Star and Dream Teamer

1. Hank Hersch, "The Shape of Things to Come," *Sports Illustrated*, November 11, 1991, pp. 131–132.

2. Frank Fortunato, *Sports Great Alonzo Mourning* (Springfield, N.J.: Enslow Publishers, Inc., 1997), p. 51.

3. Pat Jordan, "Getting Off His Shots," *The Sporting News*, December 26, 1994, p. 28.

4. Reggie Miller (with Gene Wojciechowski), *I Love Being the Enemy* (New York: Simon & Schuster, 1995), p. 280.

## Chapter 6. NBA Superstar

1. Jack McCallum, "Oh, What a Feeling!" *Sports Illustrated*, November 7, 1994, p. 104.

2. Gerry Callahan, "Floored! With Two Three-Point Thunderbolts, the Pacers' Reggie Miller Shocked the Knicks," *Sports Illustrated*, May 15, 1995, p. 27.

3. Ken Rappoport, "Reggie Miller," *Guts and Glory: Making It in the NBA* (New York: Walker and Company, 1997), p. 53.

4. Ibid., p. 54.

5. Reggie Miller (with Gene Wojciechowski), *I Love Being the Enemy* (New York: Simon & Schuster, 1995), p. 278.

## Chapter 7. Shooting in the Shadows

1. Pat Jordan, "Getting Off His Shots," *The Sporting News*, December 26, 1994, p. 28.

2. Reggie Miller (with Gene Wojciechowski), *I Love Being the Enemy* (New York: Simon & Schuster, 1995), p. 112.

3. Ibid., p. 50.

4. Mike Lopresti, "Miller Deserves Opportunity to Take Part in NBA Finals," *Lafayette (Indiana) Journal and Courier*, May 12, 1998, p. C1.

5. David Benner, (ed.), *1997–98 Official Indiana Pacers Team Yearbook* (New York: Finlay Sports, 1998), p. 40.

6. Mark Montieth, "The Bird's the Word," *MVP Pro Basketball '98* (Lombard, Ill.: MVP Media, 1998), pp. 11–12.

## Chapter 8. A Legend Playing for a Legend

1. Mark Montieth, "Shoot to Thrill," *MVP Pro Basketball '98* (Lombard, Ill.: MVP Media, 1998), p. 14.

2. Ibid.

3. Ibid.

4. David Benner, (ed.), *1997–98 Official Indiana Pacers Team Yearbook* (New York: Finlay Sports, 1998), p. 40.

5. Montieth, p. 14.

6. *Official Indiana Pacers Team Yearbook*, p. 40.

7. Dennis McCafferty, "Managing to Win," *USA Weekend*, April 24–26, 1998, p. 6.

8. Ibid., p. 5.

9. Reggie Miller (with Gene Wojciechowski), *I Love Being the Enemy* (New York: Simon & Schuster, 1995), p. 280.

10. Mike Lopresti, "Miller Deserves Opportunity to Take Part in NBA Finals," *Lafayette (Indiana) Journal and Courier*, May 12, 1998, p. C1.

# Career Statistics

| YEAR | TEAM | G | FG% | FT% | 3-PT% | REB | AST | STL | BLK | PTS | AVG |
|---|---|---|---|---|---|---|---|---|---|---|---|
| 1987–88 | Pacers | 82 | .488 | .801 | .355 | 190 | 132 | 53 | 19 | 822 | 10.0 |
| 1988–89 | Pacers | 74 | .479 | .844 | .402 | 292 | 227 | 93 | 29 | 1,181 | 16.0 |
| 1989–90 | Pacers | 82 | .514 | .868 | .414 | 295 | 311 | 110 | 18 | 2,016 | 24.6 |
| 1990–91 | Pacers | 82 | .512 | .918 | .348 | 281 | 331 | 109 | 13 | 1,855 | 22.6 |
| 1991–92 | Pacers | 82 | .501 | .858 | .378 | 318 | 314 | 105 | 26 | 1,695 | 20.7 |
| 1992–93 | Pacers | 82 | .479 | .880 | .399 | 258 | 262 | 120 | 26 | 1,736 | 21.2 |
| 1993–94 | Pacers | 79 | .503 | .908 | .421 | 212 | 248 | 119 | 24 | 1,574 | 19.9 |
| 1994–95 | Pacers | 81 | .462 | .897 | .415 | 210 | 242 | 98 | 16 | 1,588 | 19.6 |
| 1995–96 | Pacers | 76 | .473 | .863 | .410 | 214 | 253 | 77 | 13 | 1,606 | 21.1 |
| 1996–97 | Pacers | 81 | .444 | .880 | .427 | 286 | 273 | 75 | 25 | 1,751 | 21.6 |
| 1997–98 | Pacers | 81 | .477 | .868 | .429 | 232 | 171 | 78 | 11 | 1,578 | 19.5 |
| TOTALS | | 882 | .485 | .877 | .404 | 2,788 | 2,764 | 1,037 | 220 | 17,402 | 19.7 |

# Where to Write
# Reggie Miller

Mr. Reggie Miller
c/o Indiana Pacers
300 East Market Street
Indianapolis, IN 46204

**On the Internet at:**

<http://www.nba.com> (Indiana Pacers)

# Index